FUGITIVE LETTERS

FUGITIVE LETTERS

PAUL HETHERINGTON
CASSANDRA ATHERTON

Fugitive Letters
Recent Work Press
Canberra, Australia

Copyright © Paul Hetherington and Cassandra Atherton, 2020

ISBN: 9780648936756 (paperback)

 A catalogue record for this book is available from the National Library of Australia

All rights reserved. This book is copyright. Except for private study, research, criticism or reviews as permitted under the Copyright Act, no part of this book may be reproduced, stored in a retrieval system, or transmitted in any form by any means without prior written permission. Enquiries should be addressed to the publisher.

Cover image: *Le main de Madame Hugo,* 1853-1854, George Eastman Museum
Cover design: Recent Work Press
Set by Recent Work Press

recentworkpress.com

SS

PART ONE: SUDDENNESS

[Charity, 14 May 2020]

There, between rafters, like a nestled rat's hoard or hundreds of stacked insect wings—an 'affair' the size of four shoeboxes. Should I blame the workman for opening the ceiling or chide him for failing to throw those boxes out? ... A gaping suddenness—that this correspondence might still exist, sketching ghostly stories; throwing old desire into gaudy light. It's a dream woken into day, or some reconstitution of dust—will the letters vanish if I rub them between my fingers? Meandering sentences drill and rupture time.

[Charity, 15 May 2020]

The paper cracks, like one-hundred-year-old skin; sickly yellow or deathly blue: my great-aunt Birdie's stashed letters—to 'My Darling Pontificate'. Her handwriting mimics a congestion of ants, and phrases shine like snails' trails—'you named me with adoration', and 'your proposal was a reverberation'. Old cadences, like the ticking of an ornate hallway clock: 'My maid has taken cutlery—two small forks; she thinks I haven't noticed.' Birdie dips her head into a basin and her hair is 'a tangle of heavy, wild weed'. She says: 'Our love is a serpent chewing its tail.'

[Charity, 22 May 2020]

At 67, my sense of a lineage fails despite the row of frowning portraits in Birdie's original house. Even as I sort her letters, read her son's two journals, untie the frayed ribbon from Vincent's correspondence, those portraits stare me down. Fibre clings to my clumsy fingers. The censor's marks deface Vincent's letters like rubber from braking transports—three years younger than Birdie, hardly pretending to be a man, yet he served amid the Great War's lunacy. I imagine him wielding his flimsy, extravagant language while death circled, as in a monstrous abattoir: 'It's stranger than a jerking newsreel to pass a barn where eight women hang like marionettes.'

[Charity, 25 May 2020]

Birdie never married her 'Pontificate'. I searched the ceiling cavity but found nothing else—just dust and insulation. In 1932 she writes: 'Despite your ardour I won't relinquish painting. No matter what entreaties, I won't hand myself to any man'. Months later, she writes: 'and remember our in-betweenness—how we extinguish ourselves in fractured affection. Our kisses lick at impermanence.' Her words are remnants of another time; yet they still seethe with desire.

Dear Darling Pontificate,
[from Birdie, 12 February 1929]

I felt your heart as if it were a poster, advertising an elaborate drama, and your words like Guy Fawkes' rockets. After you waited an hour, professing 'to be at a loose end', you named me with adoration. Where do we find ourselves now you've departed, hardly two months into our acquaintance?

Dear DP (or Ruffian),
[from Birdie, 24 February 1929]

I may not have a 'woman's conscience' as men imagine that should be, but your lips kissed new feelings into me. Having caressed my ticklish feet, why would you question if I'm 'righteous' (even as my arching toes remember)? Despite the 'improperness' we enjoyed—that sense of toppling away from edicts—I'm 'righteous' still. I thought myself a swimming mermaid as you became like liquid. Ideas took shapes you offered me. But how can I colour what we knew? We were orange seaweed and blue sea. My canvas, staring whitely, refuses paint. We swam where I've never been.

Dear DP, or sweetly Foolish One,
[from Birdie, 17 March 1929]

Can't you hear your voice's tenor? Even in your letter it gathers pressure. Suddenly, you wish me other—and, I suppose I understand it. No man wants a woman as herself—that is, without a tether. And, yes, I abhor religion. Rich men cling to gospel while hoarding property. I was a girl of seven, sitting in the cross-branch of an oak, when a passing priest offered to chaperone me. He smiled like a medieval saint then handled me in an unholy way. His breath clicked like a speedy metronome. He took me to my mother, giving blessing. She kissed the hand that had explored my body then shouted her love of God, praying on our yard's hard ground.

Dear DP,
[from Birdie, 29 May 1929]

Yesterday I bathed in vigorous waves—I'd like to have thrown my bathing suit away. Swim into me—can I say it—as swiftly as that ocean.

Dear DP, or Complaining One,
[from Birdie, 3 June 1929]

Yes, I knew a boy once ... isn't that the start of something literary? How is it you know? In any case, he went to war and I was fully fledged in what I thought was love. We met just twice before he left. But does saying this estrange you? I kept a few of his letters—as I remember, full of stymied feeling. He dwelt in thought even when bombs were diving—and then he died. I never properly grieved—there was too much sickened aftermath of feeling. And that is all.

Dear DP, or Fearsome One,
[from Birdie, 5 December 1929]

I guess you'll visit, just as you insist. I hope we drink champagne and float into our mutual selves again. But I can't give up that boy. He's sewn into memory with sturdy thread; cutting him away would make me ragged. You say I ought to do it but you should let the dead alone. He can't step forward and kiss my hand, speaking those words he never got to say. He can't stand free and broach our feelings. Let me keep his image—poorly made of French sand and clay.

My DP,
[from Birdie, 5 February 1930]

In our tent, as the Grampians turned to purple, I thought I might dissolve. The Jaws of Death astonished me—gargantuan rocks that hold so many aeons. You turned a pebble in your hand and threw it into distance: 'I wish I might forget'. You shrugged at my inquiry but placed your hands gently on my forehead. You relented more than ever there, as if the mountain climbed within our bodies, your voice speaking like a settling rivulet. Since then, I've turned my sketches into paintings. You say your situation's 'awkward' but if you have another lover, never tell me!

[Charity, 5 June 2020]

Birdie is my image—doppelgänger, twin, my former self! If she travelled in time we'd surely merge—even her jut of nose and smile are mine. My mother said our 'similitude' was weird, and Birdie's letters are uncanny. Her words begin to dress me in fine silk—and in ball gowns of rustling taffeta. My landscape paintings start to look like hers. I imagine her pen scratching on this page, her elbow resting in this jag of sunshine.

[Charity, 11 June 2020]

So many missing letters! Did Birdie throw them out or were they stolen? I search for fugitive names and obliterated phrases, hating breaks in sequence. I strain to hear the writers breathing and isolate their motives. I occupy the intervals, trying a form of ventriloquism—attempting to reconstitute lost words. Yet Birdie remains a thousand different gestures, sliding away even as I grasp her. And as Vincent slips away in war and death, I can hardly believe the accounts he sent her—was the world he knew really such a nightmare? Meanings tantalise; forgetting is the hallmark of my reading. Identity's a tissue of lost endearments.

My DP,
[from Birdie, 5 March 1930]

There's a recent linocut by Dorrit Black. I envied it, wishing it were mine—so much the sort of thing I want to make. Yellow figures like cavorting spiders; a free, sinuous grid of lines and colours, a sense of released and shifting energy—all breaking free from male egotism. I believe it reveals a way to live—like a riff in jazz. The figures become an androgynous dance.

Dear DP,

[from Birdie, 17 April 1931]

You asked about Thea Proctor's woodblock print. It's two fond women, one offering a rose, reminding me my life belongs to women. The picture refashions the old and clichéd symbol—there's shared exchange rather than the Rose's mystic quest. And Dorrit Black's The Bridge *is salutary. She sees the world as jostling parts, as if everything we know is strangely broken. The Harbour Bridge is a symbol of discord—the world cubed and altered; unceasing loss; the future without any sure connection.*

Dear DP,
[from Birdie, 31 May 1931]

Those nudes you so admire in Rome and London—and I admire their painterly beauty, too—what do they say of civilisation, with banks collapsing and the future lost? People despair; the world begins to teeter. The old voyeurisms no longer reign, where men made their desire the theme of galleries and shows. I met the painter Dorrit Black by chance and she invited me to tea. The subject of her Nude with a Cigarette *doesn't care a fig for the gawking viewer. Her cigarette's a symbol of apartness—updating every Raphael nude.*

Dear DP,
[from Birdie, 3 June 1931]

Dreams of my son have now returned. He appears as an infant but speaks as sweetly as a novelist. Every day I think on what he says, opening tubes of paint, sitting in a paddock, painting and smelling the grass. Last week I saw an angel above a house. I watched it as I walked three city blocks. My greengrocer's boy was told to find me, handing me my forgotten purse. And still I watched the angel, asking the boy if he would dress in wings. I suppose it's madness—to care so much for what the mind's eye sees.

[Charity, 17 June 2020]

Still the past won't fully yield. Death is the blank against which these letters stand. I count them again with three new finds, hidden in the folds of others—as if notes tucked under hems; or stocking-squeezed surprises. But so many of Birdie's letters are tattered scraps—it's as if someone censored them—probably Alexander's handiwork, ruining his mother's store of memory. Birdie says in one torn fragment: 'I gather myself inside the splashing light, as if it were a room. The pure exaggeration of your gesture—if "pure" can be the word ...'

I imagine lives as artefacts—or lassoes of sentences in twisting air. I see Vincent in a mess hut staring at a letter he's received— then throwing it down, watching paper dive. It lifts in a draught and a soldier picks it up: 'You're a stupid bastard to dwell on any woman'. A gob of spit leers on the planks of the floor. The words are incommensurable.

[Charity, 28 June 2020]

Searching these letters becomes my only occupation—to stare at gaps in sequence, join ripped pages, scrutinise what has no date, quiz a censor's marks. As if each breach invites a reconstruction; as if I'm seeing these people in an ancient documentary. Vincent's Lee Enfield falls from a bench and accidentally fires. The bullet skims another soldier's ear. His commander sends him to clean out the latrines for his failure to 'make safe'. Birdie bends to gather a dropped brush and wipes a smear of vermilion from her floor. Half-way through a letter to DP, she stands and scrubs her painted canvas.

[Charity, 28 June 2020]

I remember childhood stories about our family line. We called our wealthy cousins 'The Great Achievers'. Those who died we named 'The Absent Futures'. I am someone time will forever lose, but there she is—my great-aunt, barely twenty, receiving a soldier's letters from the war. His words are agents trying to locate her, as he examines oak leaves for 'variegate forms' or holds his dignity 'as if with hands—it feels like water'. He's 'feet first deep in mud' and 'trying to hear those vanished birds'. He asks, 'are we ruined by separation?', adding, 'I'm washed by ghastliness'. He writes, 'a pipe fumes in an empty barn. I thought of my father in an easy chair, harrumphing "most obliged"'.

[Charity, 29 June 2020]

Vincent's group of letters was separate, wrapped with layers of white tissue paper and tied with purple ribbon in a bow. The workman said they had their own container which he'd thrown out—a woodworm-infested heart-shaped box. He said he may have lost some of the letters—as he threw the box away the ribboned clump had fallen. And when I look into Vincent's correspondence, it is so hard to place. Could Birdie have loved this boy?

Dear B,
[from Vincent, undated, probably 1916]

I write because there's a break in marching. A river we passed was the colour of your eyes—I hadn't expected blue water in this wasteland—before we came to a lake with ███ *floating in it. Houses are fuming.* ███████████
████████████████████████████
███████████. *There was an eight-year-old girl from the local village. I spoke to her in awkward French and she complained of the lack of birds—pointing at field and forest. I asked about her parents but, once again, 'Where are all the birds?' She thought I was a fool. There was* ██████████████████
██ *and we fell down like a herd of myotonic goats—all of us except the girl. But nothing else happened. Just silence, so eventually we stood up. She had a buoyant way of walking, like gravity didn't weigh on her, crossing the road to a broken cottage. I searched later. Inside there was a single, rickety bed, two cups, an ornate teapot and a few knick-knacks. And a leather-bound book in a strange language stashed in a wardrobe. She had scarpered but there were skilful drawings of birds pinned to the walls, almost as if perching—maybe twenty or thirty, each carefully coloured. How does the poem go: 'And this is why I sojourn here ... And no birds sing'?*

Dear B,
[from Vincent, undated, probably 1916]

Before I decamped from Australia you said we were badly suited—opposed religions, parents. And it's true. I know as much as your wealthy crowd but it's all self-taught and my accent's wrong. When I met Maisie—is she still your 'best friend'?—she heard it in my voice: Catholicism and left-wing upstart views. I suppose that's why she asked me about hunting and riding. You laughed when I said I hunted words, but she thought me gauche. And now I'm wearing ridiculous, uncomfortable clothes and kicking dust—although my love draws your image towards me as I drink you in this porcelain air. It's a version of Ivanosvsky's experiments—I filter feeling yet fail to conjure you.

Dear B,

[from Vincent, undated, probably 1916]

Your reassurance is a blessing. If my old friend, the ▮▮▮ wasn't reading this, I'd reminisce about having you in hand—and remember all is figurative where I am—that prickly grass and rise. There were two captured ▮▮▮▮▮▮▮ and my fellow soldier, a right ▮▮▮▮, when he heard they shared the same name, well, he pulled out his pistol and ▮▮▮▮▮▮▮▮▮. Just like that. So much for the ▮▮▮▮▮▮▮▮. I'd talked to them because I have some rudimentary knowledge of ▮▮▮▮. One kept talking about his mother missing him. How she would hold her hands high when praying—directing her prayers to God. Apparently, she had hair down to her waist, like you, and used to wash it in a tub, squeezing it through her hands to rinse it, as you do, and this ▮▮▮▮ said, ▮▮▮▮▮▮▮▮▮▮▮▮▮▮▮, which means, 'I always loved her for that gesture'. The other said little, but his eyes had depth, like yours, and showed his feeling. Five minutes later both lay face down.

Dear B,
[from Vincent, undated, probably 1916]

We're in the Canton of ▮▮▮▮▮▮▮▮, *which is part of Lorraine. We're not far from what was a beautiful village on a gentle slope that used to climb above a small, clean river—but it's completely gone. The locals (the few who are left) call it* un village détruit *(a destroyed village) because so many shells were dumped on this place everything was flattened. Sometimes you can find a few stones that were once a wall, but it's almost impossible to think people farmed on this poisoned ground. Picking up a stone, wiping away the grime and soil, made me think of the ideas we fight for—but all I sensed was an end.*

Dear B,
[from Vincent, undated, probably 1917]

I'm sorry for the break in writing. We had a long march and, now, digging out old trenches is most of what we do—this place is already riddled from last summer's fighting. There were so many dead some were buried upright in the trenches' sides and yesterday, when talking to a mate, I felt a hand placed firmly on my shoulder. It was one of those buried men. We've no time for proper rites—grenades, mortars and bombs fall continually. I still read my copy of Jane Eyre. *Such civilised strangeness is a comfort.*

Dear B,
[from Vincent, undated, probably 1917]

I thought of my father after a shell knocked a man down. He knew a few things—how to hoist a beer glass on the tip of one finger; how to shift my mother from her blacker moods; also the cobbling his father taught. We gathered the soldier from an open field— ▆▆▆▆▆▆ *— crumpled on a stretcher, and his moustache was my father's. Before he died he lifted his hands and asked me if I'd write to his niece (he had my father's thick fingers). I asked her name but he was already gone. My father had fought in the first Boer War and never talked of it, except to say, 'look after the women'. I saw his eyes in pieces of shrapnel.*

Dear B,
[from Vincent, undated, probably 1917]

We left the orchard I mentioned earlier, where we'd had a run-in with the locals, and entered an old château—stuck on a hillside like a huge, fractured tooth. It was made of many pasts—built in the sixteenth century on a mill site mentioned by some scribe in the eleventh century. There was a ruined monastery nearby and a soldier insisted he saw a medieval monk walking in the grounds, which made us all laugh uneasily. Inside the château there were blue-and-white Delft tiles around a large fireplace and yellow and red wallpaper hanging in strips. I imagined you as the lady of the manor when the place was resplendent, both of us lording it over this lovely piece of countryside.

Dear B,
[from Vincent, undated, probably 1917]

The locals said the château was abandoned decades ago, although an aristocratic poet apparently lived there in the seventeenth century. Two days ago I heard music, so I walked inside and a young woman was sitting at a piano in the middle of the ballroom. She was playing the first movement of the Appassionata, *rubble and dust around her feet. She'd been a concert pianist but went mad when the war started. I tried to speak to her but she wouldn't turn her head. Her fingernails were dirty and the piano keys grimy, but the music was in tune. After she finished, she left the piano stool and started doing a kind of dance, crouching like a spider as she moved.*

Dear B,
[from Vincent, undated, probably 1917]

We had a terrible journey in cattle trucks through rain to billets that would make you smile (so fond of comfort as you are). We slept on the ground in a barn, eating bully beef and a few potatoes. And drinking rum—but not in sufficient quantity!

Dear B,
[from Vincent, undated, probably 1917]

I'm writing briefly again because I haven't been well. We were sent to a scrubby, tangled wood where we laid up for a week, waiting for orders. When we moved up the hill there was a rain of shrapnel and gas shells. I breathed in too much of the stuff—it felt like I was breathing needles—and have been sent to a hospital in ■■■■. *I'm waiting for a decision—whether I go back or get sent home.*

Dear B,

[from Vincent, undated, probably 1917]

I'm in better health at last. Supply trucks lumbered past and a group of British soldiers have joined us in a barn we've requisitioned. It's overrun with rats and sometimes we wake at night as they run across our bodies. There's an old church that's lost its roof but has half its steeple. The churchyard looks like the dead have woken, with holes everywhere, most of them full of water, and exposed skeletons looking as if they'll climb out any minute. The locals, whoever they were, are gone. Not one person can be found, even though many of the houses are in good condition—but they're only inhabited by the breeze. Some are well furnished. One has carved eighteenth-century chairs, and there's a child's drawing in crayon pinned to a board. It shows a family under a massive blue sun. That house also has a rose garden blooming with reds and oranges like some Fauvist extravaganza.

Dear B,
[from Vincent, undated, 1917]

Your news astonishes. I'm completely at a loss except to say how madly wonderful. If only I could say it in person! We're back at the front being shelled and, yet, in this mayhem, I think of the child we made on that pulsing day—such unexpected news. I aim to make it through.

[Charity, 31 July 2020]

Birdie's mother gave the child away, ensuring he took another name. Later, Birdie wrote of 'his long, stern face and a cry like a kitten—or so the midwife told me. I'd have called him Henry, like an ancient king. I'd have shown him paintings and changed the complexion of my life.' After the death of his adoptive parents, Alexander sought her out—a strange encounter as his journals tell it. Then, like his father, he went to war, dying in a training mishap.

[Charity, 3 August 2020]

The truth is I nearly burnt the journals—as soon as I'd read a few messy entries (his handwriting's a scrubby hedge crammed onto the pages). But I remembered Birdie kept them and decided to honour that. She even wrapped them like some sort of gift. Before she met him she'd written: 'I've lost my form. I remember the arrival of shapelessness from the moment my son was taken. Perhaps my painting chases that body (the form I'd made in my young, swelling body). But it's not a bridgeable gap. The unspeakable saturates being.'

PART TWO: SEARCHING

[Alexander's journal entry for 30 May 1938]

Six months of searching to find my mother—'you can't be given the information you require: it's against the law'. But a gap-toothed trainee deigned to help me—encouraged by a couple of dinners, a few fond kisses, a promise or two. Then I had her in an alleyway, her back against the grimy wall and her gasps like the cry of a magpie.

Today I knocked at my mother's door. Trepidation sang like stridulating crickets, though no-one answered.

[Alexander's journal entry for 3 June 1938]

Nine thousand diamonds have been found at Valencia, and gold and silver in Rue Mouffetard. The Germans are sending Jews to Dachau and Franco is bombing the Spanish coast. But Tosca's a success at Convent Garden. Isn't that marvellous—high culture goes on! How mad the world's become!

[Alexander's journal entry for 6 June 1938]

Again, my mother wasn't there. Perhaps she's travelling or taking the cure. Or hiding because she thinks I'm a salesman. Maybe I'll dress up next time I visit—put on tails or some velvet suit, polish my accent. For years I imagined her a storied countess—with entourage, horses, venison and wine; riding side-saddle across her vast estates; issuing commands in imperious tones; being refinement's epitome. My adoptive parents claimed not to know her, but I've tracked her down like a hound at bay.

[Alexander's journal entry for 8 June 1938]

At last she answered my knock at the door, recoiling at my measured words. She asked for proof, which I refused. I said I'd returned to claim the life she'd stolen from me—or words of that kind. She looked at me as if I was a monster: 'I believed we'd never meet.' I gave a small bow, like a knight to a dame, but she continued to stare, stepping away when I tried to kiss her: 'How did you find me? Who told you where I live?'

[Alexander's journal entry for 10 September 1938]

She's relented at last: I have my room. We've not grown fond—I think she reviles me to her friends—but at last I'm home. I wander the house—a labyrinth of privilege, given (she says) by her doting mother. Paintings are everywhere like a kind of litter; a mess of making despite her prissy maid (I tried to kiss her but she slapped my face). And I disagree with her attitude—her work tries to break established rules—she'd overturn many millennia. And my scepticism angers her—she calls me 'reactionary' for loving Rembrandt's and Caravaggio's paintings. So, I overpraise the Greeks and their wonderful culture and Egyptian scarabs in lapis lazuli.

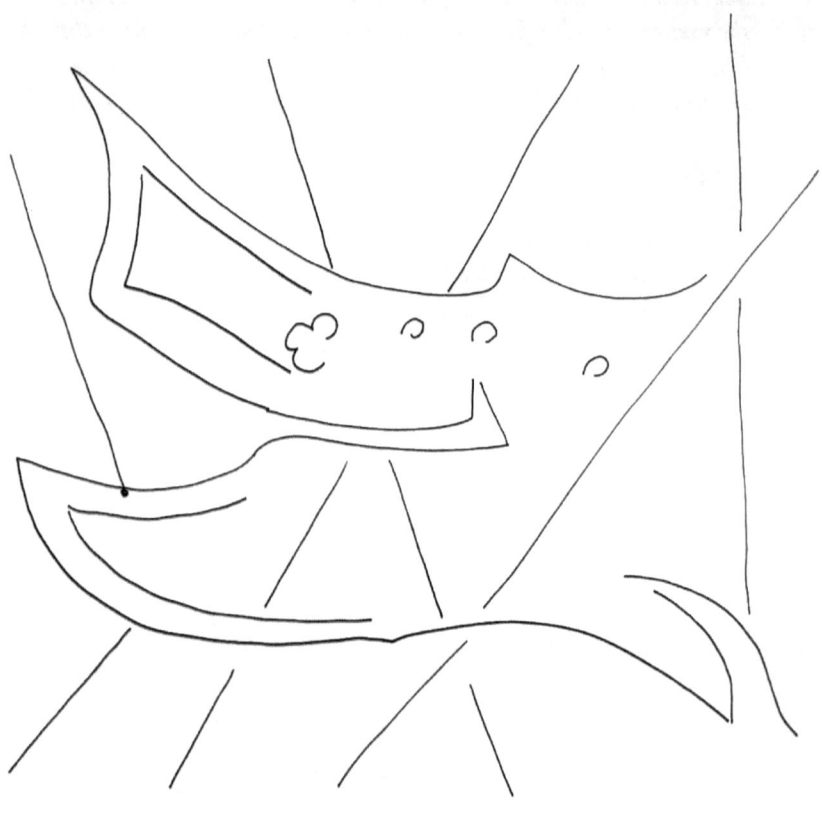

[Alexander's journal entry for 16 September 1938]

My mother's still trapped in suspicion. As if my name was never my own; as if I'm not the parcel she gave away: 'You're not as I imagined. I thought you'd be taller.' But who is she to 'imagine' me? She hates my manners because they're 'ordinary' . 'It was impossible,' she says, 'for me to keep you.'

I jemmied her desk. There's a stash of letters she wrote to 'DP', that he must have returned. I stole a bundle to read at leisure. She seems to love him but won't obey—I'd counsel her to restrain her opinions. I watch as she paints, dabbing and mixing, creating scenes—and know I won't persuade her.

[Alexander's journal entry for 16 October 1938]

Her letters upset me so I burned a handful and tore up others—it was pleasurable to break into her privacy. But then I relented and returned the rest. I suppose she's entitled to her immorality. She knew of my trespass: 'How dare you pry? Despite your claims, you're not my son. And you've no right to my private life.'

My adoptive parents were silly as birds, trying to love but without the talent—both do-gooders in their different ways. On our small lawn they fed the magpies with bits of mince. I trapped them with lassoes of the finest wire.

[Alexander's journal entry for 18 October 1938]

Britain re-arms. The world still teeters. Light, voyeur-like, stares me down. My mother paints and sometimes cooks—such elaborate, inedible meals! I grew up separately while she made love, cossetting her fine 'DP'. Now I try to make her face her failure but she barely has the nerve to do it. I'm more my father's son than hers.

I intercepted her letter to a friend and her blatant selfishness condemns me: 'I think I'll give my art away. The loss I suffered has turned to poison. My son uses my own words against me: "You'd rather be a man. Where are your natural feelings?"' I suppose it's time to consider leaving.

[Alexander's journal entry for 30 March 1939]

I stole two paintings from the attic and, in the back yard, doused them well—told her I was burning rubbish. Some ghastly views of the Grampians with small figures looking at a view—a well-dressed man and a yellow woman. They fumed and burst into pretty, coloured flame.

She paints despite the 'smash-and-grab new world'—as Eden calls it. The government makes a register of men. War, like a driverless train, approaches. Every day I think of my father. Last week my mother finally revealed his letters. He writes, 'of the child we made'.

[Charity, 8 August 2020]

Hoping to find more of Birdie's things—he mentions in his journal 'stealing what was precious'—I prised apart the stapled pages at the back of Alexander's second journal. I found some yellow ribbon, three seed beads and a series of letters from DP's wife, written in the 1970s.

Why would Birdie hide them there? Why keep them? Birdie had already suffered—those letters must have been her proverbial bitter end.

Dear Birdie,
[from Ruby, 16 December 1975]

On blue Sundays, as the church bells tolled, I'd take your most recent missive from under the mattress and live your bright moments one line at a time. I don't suppose you knew that's where he kept them—your fond DP; your coded love. It took me little time to find the meaning. You won't have realised his previous lover used a similar endearment. It was always a game to him—your Delta Pi collected lovers like trinkets. He stored their vanities of letters in a suitcase at the top of the wardrobe—which yours eventually joined. All I needed was a step ladder on a lazy afternoon ....

I enclose those letters in their torn envelopes. My fingerprints were the last to bruise their pages.

Dear Birdie,
[from Ruby, 22 December 1975]

In those years, I thought of you as a shipwreck. When you talked of orange seaweed in the blue ocean, you were already foundering. Didn't you feel the cold water lapping at the hem of your dress? In my journal, I named you Ophelia, thinking of those strange, prophetic words: 'An envious sliver broke'.

I have names for all his lovers—Queen of Hearts; Cheese Soufflé; Tuesday; Silver Feet; Miss America; Blanchefleur ... You were singing even as you drowned; were there no words to serve as watchman to your heart? While his silences pained you, your DP was warming another woman's bed. But you ask too many questions to answer in one letter. Did he ever mention you? No. But a sketch of withered violets in his hand has your initials scribbled in the bottom corner.

Dear Birdie,
[from Ruby, 2 January 1976]

He was always going to extinguish what you called your 'bonfire heart'. While you were mesmerised by his explosive words, he only saw a naked flame. He stayed while there was early passion; only lingered with you when desire's embers floated in the air. Back then you thought your DP was at a loose end, but he had enough women to fill his days.

Does it matter what I was doing then? Would you have cared if you knew of my distress? I waited for his thought's abstraction to fade like your perfume on his collar. I read Chekhov and Maupassant and looked for long, orange hairs wound around his buttons. Once, I found three and—as in the story—I threw them from the window.

Dear Birdie,
[from Ruby, 22 January 1976]

Atheism has its charms, but I wonder if every person on their deathbed doesn't end up praying. I find my consolation in the tolling of the church's bell, in confession and absolution, in knowing my sins. I'm sorry you lost your religion in the unholy grasping of a wayward priest; may he combust at the altar!

Despite his sanctimony, your DP was agnostic, so does it surprise you he was also faithless? Or do you only take unfaithfulness as seriously as your tickled feet? I have wondered if mermaids—as you claim to be—shapeshift their way into men's beds. Perhaps Tennyson knew, or Waterhouse had an inkling. In the end, you have your canvases and I have my journals. If we keep filling them with slanted truths, they may last longer than any man. Did DP tell you he liked navy blue? Make sure you add a spot of midnight to your vaunted, purpled Grampians.

Dear Birdie,
[from Ruby, 12 February 1976]

... I've also seen forest rising above the farmland and written pages about the sandstone ridges and vertiginous slopes. Once I even saw romance in the wildflowers and the waterfall, and watched the sun set over the ravine. On that day, pink flossed the skies and the waxing moon seemed fat with expectation. You say when you camped in the Grampians, he didn't tell you of his lovers or his wife. Perhaps you thought your tented intimacy was a match for nature's omnipotence?

Dear Birdie,
[from Ruby, 27 February 1976]

Of course I told him about your Vincent. I saw that letter first and opened it, speaking your names together, watching him refill his whisky glass—once, then again. Slugs of Dalwhinnie on his tongue as I repeated the description of Vincent hunting words not waterfowl and speculated on the surprising strength of your feelings for him. That night he went to bed early and I imagined your poppy-covered lover making his dreams an eerie wasteland.

...

You said you kept Vincent's letters. I hope you keep them separate. Do they smell of earthy devotion and long wakeful nights; the promise of starlit evenings and a ghastly kind of constancy?

Dear Birdie,
[from Ruby, 18 April 1976]

Did my husband place the span of his hands around your waist; his palms drawing heat and his head bending at the sweet intake of breath? Did he run his fingers against your clothed thighs? The only thing he liked more than sumptuous textiles and the snap of a tape measure was a woman's body warming the finest satin or silk. He dressed each of his lovers in a different colour; a spinning wheel of usurping desire. I know your dress was yellow satin, like buttercups and moonlight—or, I must say it, yellow-bellied desire. Your DP had matching pocket squares laid out in our wardrobe. The yellow square has remnants of silver eyeshadow—if held closely to the light.

Dear Birdie,
[from Ruby, 22 June 1976]

I'm not sure how knowing he dressed me in green silk can be any salve for your memory— as you seem to suggest. 'Evergreen,' he said when he first took the gown out of the box and slipped it over my head. If it helps, you were the youngest and prettiest—the one who jagged in him, like a kind of burr. Sometimes in the mornings, when steam fogged the bathroom mirror, he'd stare at his smudged outline. In those moments, I thought you had changed him a little; made him question the shape of things. Not for long, though. While he'd never have left me, occasionally when we were together, I could tell he was reliving desire's yellow memories.

Dear Birdie,
[from Ruby, 27 July 1976]

Yes, some of it was your debate about beauty. Writing to him about Modernist art—the tutelage involved. It angered and fascinated and titillated him. He'd previously thought of his lovers as carnival kewpie dolls on sticks— and you were always wriggling free. He loved the Elgin Marbles *and draped female figures— you won't be surprised to know he could stand for hours admiring sculpted falls of fabric. His idea of 'modern' art was Baily's* Eve Listening to the Voice—*especially the perfection of her outstretched index finger. Dorrit Black's art was too much for him—he couldn't make the leap. I suppose your DP was a gazer; the quintessential beholder of a fixed idea of beauty. Your generation can see beauty in fracture. Try to think more softly of him and forgive his rigidity—as I will try to do. (How sad it was to read of Black's death all those years ago, knowing you once had tea with her.)*

Dear Birdie,
[from Ruby, 12 August 1976]

When I posted my previous letter, I was convinced it was my last. As it settled onto the other notes and cards in the post box, I thought our correspondence was over—you would keep your memories and I'd go back to curating my sense of 'afterwards'—reimagining his life without lovers and showing an abiding faithfulness.

But now I've happened across more of your letters—as if I can't escape his scraps of former feeling; as if his fond detritus will forever catch at me. I send them on as a gesture of good will, although your letters make me an unhappy voyeur.

Lately, in my dreams, I see a black-haired child I believe to be your son. He's dressed in corduroy and has red cheeks. He gestures at an empty boat moored to a broken pier—and, just before I wake, he hands me an overflowing bucket of sand.

Dear DP,
[from Birdie, 1 July 1931]

Last night I dressed in the yellow satin gown you bought, laying your hands all over me. (I laugh to think of it and hope you might appear again with such conspicuous lack of self-control.) In any case, I went to an awful party and talked to twenty people. I used to enjoy the dance of words, and how my beauty captivated strangers. But the egotism's left me. Three men suggested dinner and I couldn't imagine pushing food about my plate while being ogled. They were the sort that love a 'female artist'. One spoke of the 'fairer sex'—can you imagine!

Dear DP,
[from Birdie, 11 December 1931]

I cannot argue with you over art. You say you see no purpose in it—good! You say commerce raises everyone. You claim civilisation saves us from the primitive and talk of the value of running water.

You seem to imagine me as a child. Every morning, I wake with a single thought—to find myself through painting; to daub myself—if you get the rough idea—as if paint is blood. On the canvas, my blood is shouting out.

Dear DP,
[from Birdie, 3 January 1932]

No, I don't need 'help'. Doctors aren't equipped to understand me, unless they've painted and felt their blood explode. (Except, I knew a doctor who studied art and left his practice to work in Mexico. His savings funded programs for the poor; he wrote to me about his handmade paper.) But let's not argue over this. I cannot value convention's view of women, tying them to a banal idea of beauty; naming them gossips despite their grand ideas. I've no time for beauty when I'm painting—or not the kind that men admire in women. But, tell me, are you coming in the spring? Will we travel to the mountains?

Dear DP,

[from Birdie, 9 January 1932]

You are increasingly brief. Are you too busy to write as once you did? I always liked the passage of your thought, moving as if through highs and lows. I wish I could agree with you more often. I cherish the walks we took and your hands upon me. But I sense us moving into different spheres (I cannot be corralled or I would die). These ordered, pretty streets are bad enough—I cannot adopt a man's name as well.

Dear DP,
[from Birdie, 23 January 1932]

I have been dipping my hair into a basin, remembering my mother's hands. She used to gather my hair like laundry, lowering it into suds. Her breath was often on my face, smelling of almonds and sugar. As she leaned over me and washed, she'd sing. I remember one day turning—I was seven—and holding her as tightly as I could, feeling her breasts against my body. I wondered: 'what's it like to be a woman? When will I eat almonds mixed with sugar?' My hair was a tangle of heavy, wild weed.

Dear DP,

[from Birdie, 3 February 1932]

Why write of what we cannot change? Love, such as we have, is not the love of spouses and lives outside of bounds. I cannot bridle you; and you would surely never want to break me. How do I explain it better? You named me with adoration and I took you at your word—as I was, solitary and irreverent. Last year, your proposal was a reverberation. Yet, now our love is a serpent chewing its tail. How else to characterise the round-and-round? I tried to charm the snake but fear I've failed.

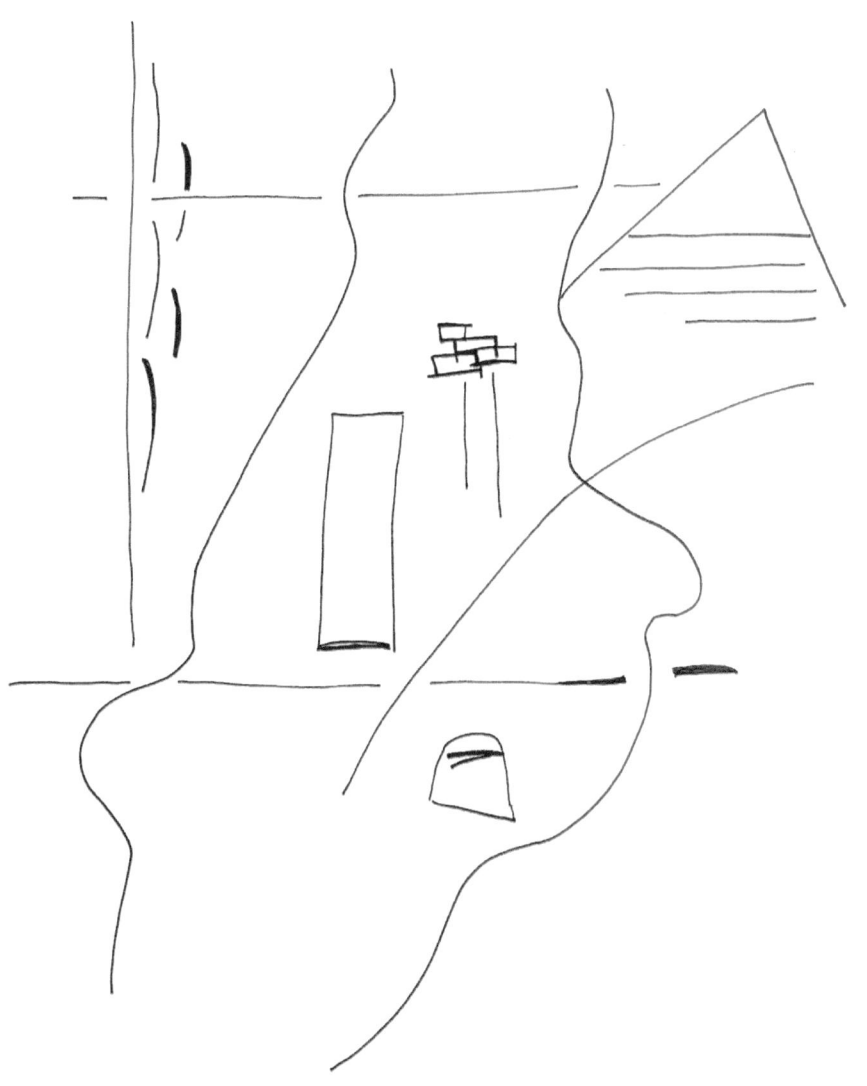

Dear DP,
[from Birdie, 28 February 1932]

You write of our diminishing connection. I feel it as an unfailing electric charge. 'Express all you are,' you said three years ago—perhaps you're dismayed I took you at your word. I suppose this is our final to-and-fro but perhaps one day you'll let me know your life—what you chose; what you thought important. For three years, I imagined that was me—another of my grand notions! Take care and I'll remember your 'devoted'.

Dear Birdie,
[from Ruby, 20 December 1976]

Thank you for your letters. I'm sorry my silence wasn't a respite. I needed to break our patchwork correspondence—I stitched your words into my own design.

I wanted nothing to do with my husband's lovers—as I said, I hated the thought of his hands all over you. But now he's gone, I suppose it hardly matters—and, in many ways, your writing animates him. It's as if I see you standing in my shoes; as if you offer a ventriloquism that strangely speaks for me.

And, to answer your earlier question, I don't think you were naïve to believe in him—he was persuasive, even to the last.

Dear Birdie,
[from Ruby, 3 January 1977]

I can't speak of having sons; we had three daughters. Sadly, he was King Lear in our family. Our second proudly reminded us her middle name was Regan. We were thinking of Geoffrey of Monmouth when we named her— that old story of the Kings of England (though, given my time again, I'd choose another name).

On quiet evenings his absence was resonant—in the ticking of the mantle clock; in the songs we sang together—old folk tunes that conjured a difference. My daughters usually stayed long after dinner, playing the piano, filling the house with dreams and melancholy. Later, they looked for faithful men and failed. Our eldest even married a libertine and left him six months after their lavish wedding. She must have wondered why I hadn't done the same.

Dear Birdie,
[from Ruby, 23 January 1977]

Yesterday, I found two more of your letters in his nightstand stashed beneath his copy of The Great Gatsby *and the Tiffany cufflinks I bought for an anniversary. I hope these are the very last. Absurdly, there are even daisies scribbled on the envelopes. I enclose them now. What does it mean to paint like a man and have paintings sharing your pulse and heartbeat? You talked of feminism while sharing my husband's bed. What of women's solidarity? Blue stockings surely clash with scarlet letters—even within your extensive palette.*

Dear DP,
[from Birdie, 6 September 1931]

What are womanly feelings? You speak of them as if I know them. But feelings do not wear a dress or trousers. My desire is very like a man's. I paint with the same devotion as a man. I formulate convictions as men must do, creating my own perspectives. And because I paint and cannot love my son, he thinks I am 'unnatural'.

After he was taken from my keeping I gave up the lies of 'proper decency'. It stole the life I wanted and rebuked me. It told me my decisions weren't my own. It tried to fence me in with admonition. If I'd been poorer, ruin must have followed. It's only family money that has saved me.

Dear DP,
[from Birdie, 27 September 1931]

Well, you may not see my point, but art's the thing that's mine alone. No manners are required when I paint and I don't need to respond to conversation. The brush extends my language into silence, which answers in blameless colours. There isn't any price for breathing air. My paintings share my pulse—I hear my heartbeat in them. Even after decades, I see my mind reflected. I know myself through looking at their forms.

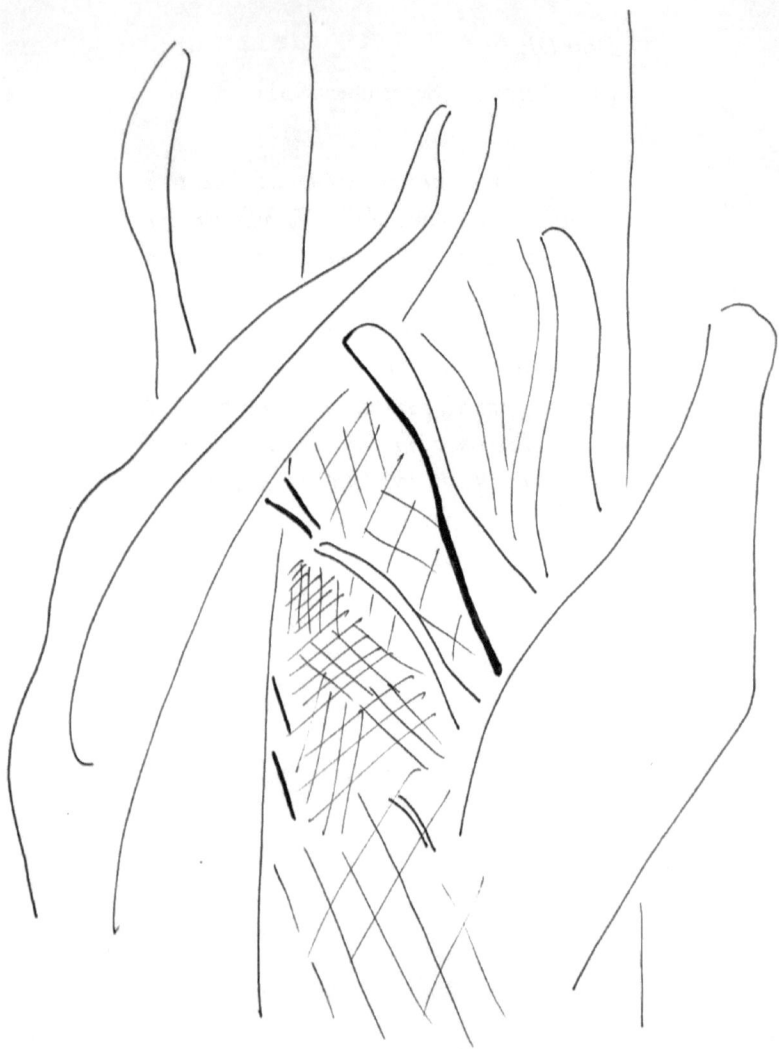

Dear Birdie,
[*from Ruby, 27 January 1977*]

I'm sorry for my recent letter. I spoke of solidarity but was antagonistic. He's gone, and I'll keep my harsh words to myself. Perversely, writing to you still conjures him; it's as if his absence in this too-large house might be temporary and he'll return with chocolates in a heart-shaped box and emerald earrings wrapped in silver paper.

In many ways he was a sentimentalist, loving moonlight walks and mountain air. I liked to pick flowers to press in scrapbooks. Always he strode ahead. Did he ever kiss you under flowering fruit trees? The falling petals were a marvellous, sweet confetti.

Dear Birdie,
[from Ruby, 1 February 1977]

Yes, it was unsettling to read of his proposal but I can't answer what his intentions were. Hold it close.

If you had married, he would soon have been an absent figure haunting your empty house—you would have passed time reading other women's letters in your yellow nightgown. The ouroboros symbolises your achievement—a stubborn kind of rebirth.

Dear Birdie,
[from Ruby, 10 February 1977]

... I can't imagine carrying a child to term only to have that child taken. Was he never laid on your body, even for a moment? I can imagine your dreams of him, the milk still in your breasts, the iron smell of birth. Children change our bodies, as you know—our bones move and never quite return.

Dear Birdie,
[from Ruby, 20 February 1977]

I'd like to invite you to afternoon tea. I'm not Dorrit Black or Emmeline Pankhurst but I can make marvellous lemon drizzle cake—one of DP's favourites, his mother's recipe. You can explain painting and bring your seven recent sketches and I'll show you the scrapbooks I've recently made.

Dear Birdie,
[from Ruby, 6 March 1977]

I've hung your painting over his favourite green chair. The shapes remind me of late summer's sun.

[Charity, 29 August 2020]

This must be the painting—Birdie had it stored in her studio behind a box. A self-portrait in reds, golds and yellow; a striking woman in her thirties. She's looking sidelong, concealing herself from the viewer's gaze despite the portrait's gesture at revelation. I, too, would hide from the staring world. In the painting's background, a photograph flattens on a desk—a man in formal dinner suit. He holds a ring and reaches outside the frame. In the painting's bottom corner Birdie's hand conceals a paintbrush.

Afterword

This collaborative sequence of prose poetry explores the relationship of the present to the past, the importance and fragility of archival materials, the beguiling force of memory and various (often negative) views of women and their roles that were far too prevalent in the twentieth century (some of which unfortunately remain). This sequence also treats a range of other themes, many of them connected to ideas of representation, history and identity, and ways of understanding familial and other intimate relationships.

Acknowledgements

While *Fugitive Letters* is a creative work, in writing it we drew on a selection of archival material to inform our prose poems about the First World War. This includes material from the National Archives (UK) and the Imperial War Museums (UK). We gratefully acknowledge those institutions and the letter writers whose work is in their collections. We mention Thea Proctor (1879–1966) and Dorrit Black (1891–1951), who are both important Australian visual artists. There are also passing references to the short story, 'A Ghost' by Guy de Maupassant and William Shakespeare's *Hamlet*. There are brief allusions to John William Waterhouse's painting *A Mermaid* (1900) and the poem, 'The Mermaid' by Alfred Tennyson. We would like to thank our partners, Michelle Hetherington and Glenn Moore, for their support and encouragement. We are grateful to Shane Strange and Recent Work Press for publishing this work.

About the authors

Paul Hetherington is a distinguished poet who has published numerous full-length poetry and prose poetry collections and has won or been nominated for more than 30 national and international awards and competitions. He won the 2014 West Australian Premier's Book Awards (poetry), was shortlisted for the 2017 Kenneth Slessor Prize and undertook an Australia Council Residency at the BR Whiting Studio in Rome in 2015–16. Paul is Professor of Writing in the Faculty of Arts and Design at the University of Canberra, head of the International Poetry Studies Institute (IPSI), and joint founding editor of the international online journal *Axon: Creative Explorations*. He founded the International Prose Poetry Group in 2014. With Cassandra Atherton, he is co-author of *Prose Poetry: An Introduction* (Princeton University Press, 2020) and co-editor of *Anthology of Australian Prose Poetry* (MUP, 2020).

Cassandra Atherton is a widely anthologised prose poet and an expert on prose poetry. She was a Visiting Scholar in English at Harvard University and a Visiting Fellow at Sophia University, Tokyo. She is the recipient of national and international research grants and awards and has judged numerous poetry awards including the Victorian Premier's Prize for Poetry, the joanne burns award and the Lord Mayor's Prize for Poetry. Cassandra's books of prose poetry include *Exhumed* (2015), *Trace* (2015), *Pre-Raphaelite* (2018) and *Leftovers* (2020). She is an Associate Professor of Writing and Literature at Deakin University and commissioning editor for *Westerly* magazine, *Axon: Creative Explorations* journal and series editor for publisher Spineless Wonders. With Paul Hetherington, she is co-author of *Prose Poetry: An Introduction* (Princeton University Press, 2020) and co-editor of *Anthology of Australian Prose Poetry* (MUP, 2020).

www.ingramcontent.com/pod-product-compliance
Lightning Source LLC
Chambersburg PA
CBHW020328010526
44107CB00054B/2028